TECH GIRLS™

$$y = x^2$$

$$A = \int_a^b f_{(x)}\, dx$$

Careers for

TECH GIRLS IN

MATH

GINA HAGLER

ROSEN
PUBLISHING®
New York

Published in 2016 by The Rosen Publishing Group, Inc.
29 East 21st Street, New York, NY 10010

Copyright © 2016 by The Rosen Publishing Group, Inc.

First Edition

Library of Congress Cataloging-in-Publication Data

Hagler, Gina, author.
Careers for tech girls in math / Gina Hagler. -- First edition.
        pages cm.—(Tech girls)
Audience: Grades 7 to 12.
Includes bibliographical references and index.
ISBN 978-1-4994-6101-5 (library bound)
1. Mathematics—Vocational guidance--Juvenile literature. 2. Mathematicians—Juvenile literature. I. Title.
QA10.5.H34 2016
510.23—dc23

                                                                                              2014043134

Manufactured in the United States of America

CONTENTS

Introduction

I t may sound silly—it's certainly difficult for most women to understand—but mathematics has historically been seen as a career field for men only. Why not women, too? Because traditional wisdom has it that girls and women are not good at math. Given the many math-related achievements by women you'll read about in these pages, you'll quickly see that this is simply not true. Women are just as good in math as men. Women also find careers in mathematics to be rewarding, challenging, and worthy of their time and energy. The "math is not for girls" stereotype is definitely one that was not only incorrect from the start, it has undoubtedly outlived its usefulness!

Danica McKellar is one woman who has already disproven the stereotype that math is just for men. She's also working to disprove a related stereotype—that a "math girl" must be unattractive or an unappealing "math nerd." McKellar is an American actress who played the role of Winnie Cooper on *The Wonder Years* and Elsie Snuffin in the fourth season of *The West Wing*. She's appeared in several other television shows, as well as on *Dancing with the Stars*.

McKellar is also a mathematician who graduated from UCLA summa cum laude with a degree in mathematics. The *British Journal of Physics* and the *New York Times* have honored her for her work as coauthor of a mathematical physics theorem known as the Chayes-McKellar-Winn theorem. She is a three-time

Danica McKellar is an American actress, mathematician, and author who believes that math is for girls and that "Smart is sexy!"

best-selling *New York Times* author, a mom, and an advocate of the ideas that "Smart is sexy!" and that girls who love math don't have to be "math nerds."

McKellar says on her website that it fits her personality to be both an entertainer and a mathematician because each role appeals to a different aspect of her personality. In a 2011 blog post, she reacted to a magnet offered by the store Forever 21. The magnet said, "I'm Too Pretty to Do Math." After suggesting some alternative slogans, McKellar wrote, "I mean, really? We're still promoting the idea that somehow looks and smarts are mutually exclusive . . . It's like we're living in the Stone Age with regard to these stereotypes."

McKellar isn't the only woman who is not ashamed to proclaim her love of math and make the best of her ability in mathematics. One of the 2014 winners of the most prestigious prize in mathematics, the Fields Medal, is a woman. The first person to effectively use a pie chart was a woman. Women played key roles in the early days of computer science. In fact, women have played important roles in math and other STEM (science, technology, engineering, and mathematics) fields throughout time.

So what does it take to be a woman in the field of mathematics? First, you need to be confident in yourself and your abilities. Then, you need to seek out opportunities to gain the experience you need. Finally, you need a commitment to lifelong learning so you can remain current with advances in your chosen field. The pages that follow will tell you more.

Chapter one

MAKING IT BIG IN MATH: CAREER FIELDS

Mathematics is an excellent career field because it includes so many different opportunities. Mathematical skills and a love of numbers can be used when pursuing a career as an educator, a financial analyst, or a manager of a fleet of cars or ships. A facility with numbers can also be used to tell a story, spot a pattern, or imagine things that are currently not possible.

For years, girls were not encouraged to take the same rigorous mathematics classes as boys because it was believed women were not as good in math as men. As a result, girls entering college lacked the knowledge base needed for the courses required in disciplines like engineering and the sciences.

Recent studies have proven that girls are just as good in math as boys—if not better. The stereotype that they are not dates back to a generation when many women didn't pursue careers outside the home or even attend college. At that time, it was also nearly unheard of for a woman to pursue a career in a math-related field. We now recognize that women's perceived incompetence in mathematics was due to their inadequate preparation in the subject.

The stereotype that girls are not good in math dates back to a time when most girls did not go on to college. Of those who did, virtually none went into math-related fields.

Today, boys and girls are exposed to a variety of mathematical concepts from an early age. Girls are expected to perform as well in math as boys with the predictable outcome that some girls will have an aptitude for and interest in math while some girls will not. That's no different than the case with boys. What is different is that girls today are more likely than ever before to be encouraged to seek help with concepts they don't understand so that they can go on to be successful in mathematics and pursue careers in related fields.

THE GLASS CEILING

For years, women have been bumping their heads on the glass ceiling—an unofficial career limit that isn't applied equally. A glass ceiling isn't written about in corporate handbooks or discussed at new employee orientations. There are no policies in place that spell out who is subject to this limitation or what needs to be done to work around it. It's a limit that exists because of tradition, stereotypes, or prejudice.

For women, the glass ceiling is one important factor that determines how far they can rise at a company or in a chosen field. For years, the glass ceiling meant there were no female Supreme Court justices, senators, chief financial officers, or chief executive officers.

The glass ceiling is still a source of frustration today because it's difficult to overcome an obstacle that isn't acknowledged. To break the glass ceiling, a woman must be an effective advocate for herself.

MATH-RELATED CAREERS

Pursuing a career in math doesn't require sitting at a calculator all day. Many who work in mathematical careers work with statistics or financial reports. Some evaluate the risk in different types of investments. Others use numbers to determine which sector of a market is doing well, how quickly a disease is spreading, whether practices that have been put in place are resulting in better quality, or what the data collected in a census tells about a population.

Women can pursue a career in many fields of math. Teaching is one of them.

Those in math-related careers may work in the fields of computer science or cryptology. Mathematics educators work at all levels of the education system, from pre-K right on through the graduate level. There are also professionals using math for research and to create theories that test the limits of what we currently know. Still others make use of their mathematical prowess to create models that make it simpler to manage large groups of items efficiently.

ADVOCATING FOR YOURSELF

Advocating for yourself is an essential part of doing well in your career. A woman who advocates for herself is not being aggressive or pushy. She is being proactive and speaking up for herself—whether that involves asking for a raise, investigating opportunities that will add to her skill set, joining associations and seeking to head committees, or asking for tuition assistance for courses that are relevant to her field.

A woman who advocates for herself effectively is confident in her abilities. Since she knows that she is in charge of her career, she has a career plan and works to gain the required experience. When she makes a request, she backs it up with related information that provides support for that request. She is a hard worker who is respected by her peers, sought after as a mentor, recognized in her field, and successful in creating a satisfying career.

PLAN OF STUDY

Preparation for a career in mathematics begins in high school, if not before, with classes that include algebra I and II, geometry, pre-calculus, and calculus. Students may also take the most rigorous AP math courses that can count for college credit. Some school systems begin high school mathematics for eligible students in middle school. Check with your guidance counselor to see what is possible.

Straight mathematics courses are not the only courses that will prepare you for further study in mathematics. Many high schools offer accounting, engineering, chemistry, physics, and statistics

It's important for girls to take rigorous math classes. Some of the material will make sense right away. Some of it will not. That's just the same as it is for boys.

courses. Each of these makes use of math. It may also be possible to take classes in marketing or sociology. These classes interpret the numbers included in reports.

Some high schools have signature programs in math. In these programs, there are stringent requirements for the classes and related classes that must be completed. AP coursework is also often required. Some school systems have magnet schools for mathematics. There is generally a test for admission. Those who score within the range and cannot have their needs met at their high school may be able to attend. Magnet programs in math and science often include classes in discrete mathematics, linear algebra, and complex analysis. If your high school doesn't offer these types of classes, check with your guidance counselor to see if it's possible to take them for credit at your community college.

If you're not sure you're ready for all of these math classes, don't worry. Start at the beginning and see where your interests and ability take you. Don't give up if you need help to master some of the concepts. The most important thing is to get the basics of algebra and geometry. These two disciplines will be used over and over again throughout your math career.

You can check with prospective colleges, association sites, or the career counselor at school to learn which math classes are required for the college major you're considering. You will likely need to complete college-level classes in the math you took in high school. You will also take probability and statistics. Your electives may include sampling theory, partial differential equations, or thermodynamics—it will depend upon the specific major.

STATISTICS AND FINANCE: USING NUMBERS TO TELL A STORY

Those with careers in statistics and finance use numbers to tell a story. It might be the story of how well one group is doing in a subject versus another. It might be the story of which branch of a company is struggling and which is not. Professionals in these fields are not only able to tell a story with numbers, they are able to interpret the numbers to learn about what's happening. In this way, a page of numbers and percentages is analyzed and interpreted before an explanation using the numbers is shared with others. It's the job of the statistician or financial analyst to present her findings in a way that is accessible to the audience for the results.

STATISTICS

The American Statistical Association (ASA) defines statistics as "the science of learning from data, and

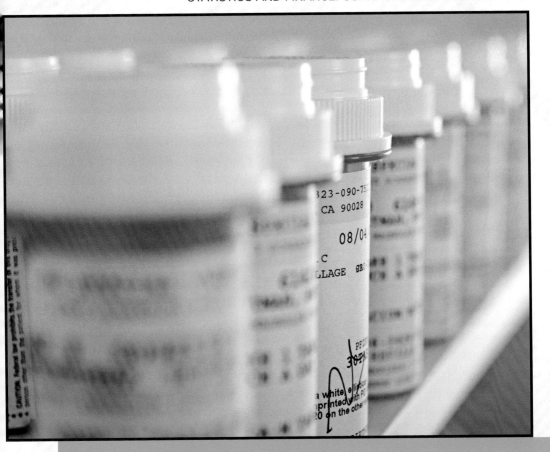

323-090-7
CA 90028

08/04

.C
LLAGE

Statistics play a key role in the pharmaceutical industry, where new drugs must undergo thorough testing before being brought to market.

of measuring, controlling, and communicating uncertainty . . ." Statisticians apply their methods to questions and problems in business, science, and public health. It's up to them to decide which factors should be examined, how large the sample should be, and how results will be tabulated and shared with others.

Medicine is one field that utilizes statisticians. Before a new drug or medication can be brought to the market, a series of trials—tests—must be performed. The last of the trials is performed on humans. Data is collected to see how well those taking the medication do compared to people with similar characteristics who didn't receive the medication. Statistics are used to compare the study to other studies that have been done or are underway. By using the data to produce meaningful statistics, a great deal of information can be effectively studied and shared.

Other fields that employ statisticians are agriculture, engineering, manufacturing, and insurance. In the insurance field, actuaries use figures about life expectancy under a variety of circumstances to set rates for insurance policies. In agriculture, engineering, and manufacturing, statistics are used to assess the success of different types of crops, the effectiveness of new engineering systems, and the success of changes in the manufacturing process. The government employs statisticians for work related to the census, public health, and the criminal justice system. It is their work that helps to determine the course of public policy.

To become a statistician, you must complete coursework in English, mathematics, and computer science in high school. These are important so that you'll know how to write a report, calculate the necessary figures, and make use of a computer for research and calculations. In college you'll need to take classes in statistics and applied mathematics. Some positions will require a master's degree or more. You can see what's required for what you'd like to do by looking at the requirements for various degrees on a university website. Be sure also to consult the ASA website.

FLORENCE NIGHTINGALE AND SANITARY REFORM THROUGH STATISTICS

Florence Nightingale was not only the founder of modern nursing, she was the first to use a pie chart to make her numbers easier to understand. According to her statistics, more soldiers were killed by cholera, typhus, and dysentery during the Crimean War

(continued on the next page)

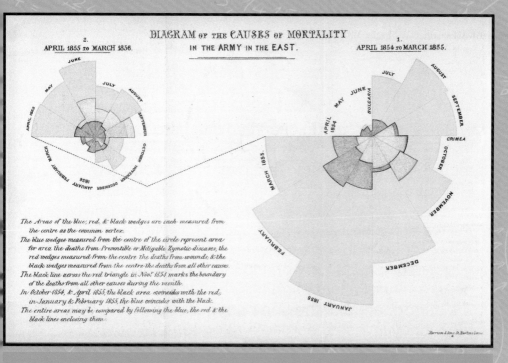

Florence Nightingale's use of these charts helped to bring about changes in hospitals worldwide.

(continued from the previous page)

(1853–1856) than were killed during battle. Nightingale wanted to bring better sanitary practices to military hospitals. To do that, she needed the people reading her reports to understand just how serious the situation was.

Nightingale created a pie chart with a slice for each month. The more deaths that occurred that month, the farther that slice of the pie stuck out. Each slice also had a section for deaths from wounds, "other causes," and disease. It was easy to see that disease killed more soldiers than any other cause. Something had to be done to improve conditions in the military hospitals if the men were to survive.

FINANCE

Those with a career in finance make use of the numbers prepared by others. They may receive reports from accounting, an investment company, or individuals seeking credit. In their role as a financial adviser or analyst, they use the numbers they receive to "read" the story told by those numbers. The story the numbers tell is the basis for their decision.

A financial analyst working in the treasury department of a large firm may be required to assess the performance of the company's investments. Has the money invested earned a good return? How does that return compare to that earned by others? Was the return worth the risk? What alternative investments might have been made? Were there other uses of that money that would have gained returns that were more beneficial to the company?

A financial adviser works with a couple to discuss their current finances, future goals, and tolerance for risk in their investments.

A financial adviser working with an individual or couple performs a similar function. The difference is that the adviser will use the results of the individual's or couple's investments. Loan officers look at an applicant's credit history to decide whether or not a loan is a good use of the bank's or credit union's money. The rate to be charged on the loan will also be decided based upon the loan officer's assessment of the numbers.

Financial analysts are also involved when a company or government agency must decide between two projects that require a large investment. By using their skills with numbers, financial analysts examine the total costs, all the risks, and the other options open for those funds. When their analysis is complete, they present their findings to the people who will make the final decision.

USING ENERGY RETURN ON INVESTMENT TO EVALUATE ALTERNATIVE ENERGY SOURCES

The results of financial models such as ROI and EROI are invaluable to decision makers faced with choosing between attractive investment opportunities.

The return on investment (ROI) considers all the costs, including interest, associated with a project. This is done for each proposed project and investment. The results are then compared to the ROI of all other possible projects to determine which is the best use of the money available.

The energy return on investment (EROI) is used to evaluate the true costs associated with the production of energy. It considers both the monetary and energy inputs that go into the production of a kilowatt-hour or a gallon of gas. By using the EROI it's possible to look at the energy that goes into the energy that comes out. With this knowledge, decision makers can decide whether an attractive alternative energy source is actually spending more energy that it creates.

To major in finance, you must take classes in statistics, business management, finance, economics, and accounting. The accounting classes are essential to your understanding of the financial statements you will study when determining the health of a company. The statistics and finance classes will prepare you for your work with numbers. Economics classes will give you the necessary understanding in the way different segments of the economy or a company work together. There are also many certifications that will qualify you for specific work as you progress in your career.

COMPUTER SCIENCE AND CRYPTOLOGY: SPOTTING PATTERNS

Computer science and cryptology are two mathematical careers that involve the use of patterns. Computer scientists create computer programs, also known as algorithms, to help spot patterns in data. In cryptology, a message is hidden in a code. The basis of this code is the pattern that is used to create and decipher the message. Cybersecurity—the type of security used to keep information safe on electronic devices and the Internet—is also based upon a pattern. The trick is that the pattern must be complex enough not to be easily broken.

COMPUTER SCIENCE

Computer science professionals use a branch of mathematics known as logic in their work. They do not build the physical systems; their job is to create the software that will make the hardware work together in the desired way. They do this by writing programs to perform tasks and calculations. These programs are often part of larger systems.

Some computer scientists work in AI (artificial intelligence). They model human thought patterns with the goal of eventually creating programs with the capacity to learn and adapt. Expert systems are a form of AI that is used to help with diagnosis. Symptoms are entered, and the program asks for additional information or returns a list of potential illnesses.

Computer scientists also work in the field of robotics. The computer scientist isn't the person building the robot or its circuits. The computer scientist is the person writing the programs that instruct robots. These robots are not like the robots in the movies. They don't roam around on their own. Robots today are used on the

A computer scientist writes the programs that control the operation of robotic arms like this one.

assembly line to perform specific tasks, like attaching a car door to its hinges or testing various components of a mechanical system. They may even speak. When they do, the tasks they perform will be determined by their programming.

A career in computer science may be a good fit for you if you enjoy working through a problem step by step. As you pursue a degree in computer science, you must complete a number of logic and programming courses

GRACE HOPPER, THELMA ESTRIN

When computers were first invented, instructions were given and results were delivered in binary code: strings of 0s and 1s. It made communicating with a computer very tedious. The first computer language—a way to communicate with the computer in words rather than digits—was created in 1947 by mathematical genius Rear Admiral Grace Hopper. By doing this, she forever changed the way we relate to computers.

Dr. Thelma Estrin was awarded a 1977 IEEE Life Fellow "for contributions to the design and application of computer systems for neurophysiological and brain research." One of the pioneers in the field of biomedicine, she performed studies of EEG readings in people with epilepsy. In her acceptance speech for the Society of Women Engineers, Estrin said that she did not know a woman engineer until she became one herself.

It's fortunate that these women had the confidence to pursue their passion in math.

at the college level. As you fulfill the requirements for the major, you are able to take elective courses. During these electives, you may discover that writing systems and programs for biomedical devices is the specialty that appeals most to you. It may be that creating software systems for equipment used in the space program or the programs behind smart presentation screens used in school is more your thing. It could be that creating video games or navigation systems is what you'd like to do. Or, it could be that you want to write computer programs to support those looking for answers to the secrets of the universe.

CRYPTOLOGY

Cryptology is a highly specialized field. Cryptologists use codes, puzzles, or cryptograms to protect information. That information may belong to a government, a business, or an individual. Whichever it is, the cryptologist uses her skillset to make the code protecting that information as difficult to crack as possible. A cryptologist also uses her skillset to crack the code on information belonging to entities that may wish to do harm to a government, business, or individual.

Governments use cryptologists to encode sensitive information. It may be as simple as the travel plans for the president or as complicated as the design of a new weapons system. It may also be as routine a task as encoding the information that is used to deliver Social Security and other government payments to recipients. In each situation, a cryptologist, or team of cryptologists, will decide upon the precise details and the exact code. Because many samples of a code may make it easier to crack, codes are changed frequently.

These cryptology technicians are checking the encrypted signal being sent by an aircraft carrier.

Businesses also use cryptologists to encode sensitive information. This may include the information given to them when a customer applies for a credit card. It may include the information captured during a debit or credit card transaction. It may also include the deposits made to the bank at the end of each day. None of this is information that is public. All of it is private. It is essential that this information is kept secure, especially as it travels over computer networks that are not under the control of the business. To ensure this, the information is encrypted. The information won't

THE WOMEN OF BLETCHLEY PARK

During World War II, Bletchley Park mansion in England was home to a team known as the Codebreakers. Members of this team were recruited because they were either in the military, were from families known by the British government to be trustworthy, or could complete a difficult crossword puzzle in less

(continued on the next page)

The women of Bletchley Park were mostly young. Many were amazingly fast at solving puzzles.

(continued from the previous page)

than twelve minutes. The Codebreakers were tasked with breaking the codes used by the enemies of the Allied forces.

The entire operation was classified and kept secret, but we know today that the Codebreakers were very successful. They were even able to use their knowledge of Hitler's codes to send him disinformation and throw him off the track on D-Day! We also know that nearly 90 percent of these essential workers were young women and teenage girls who were summoned by letter, reported to Bletchley Park, and performed a job that helped to shorten the war by nearly two years.

be useful unless both the sending and receiving party have the proper information in place.

If you enjoy puzzles, cryptograms, and ciphers, a career in cryptology might be just right for you. You will need to major in math, computer science, or information technology. You may be able to take some classes in cryptology at the undergraduate level, but most of your coursework in cryptology will be done at the graduate level.

EDUCATING OTHERS: SHARING YOUR LOVE OF MATH

ome say teachers are born. Others say teachers are made. Whatever the case, if you love to share an elegant solution or explain the way a problem in mathematics works, a career as a math educator could be perfect for you. Math teachers work in preschools, elementary schools, middle schools, and high schools, and at the university level. They are the people who bring mathematical concepts to life for their students by sharing their passion for math.

You can pursue a career as a teacher by earning a degree in education with an emphasis in math. You may also be able to earn a degree in mathematics and then complete coursework that will qualify you to teach. Check with your local school district to see its requirements. These requirements may differ depending upon the grades you plan to teach. Certification and licensing requirements vary by state, so be certain to see what you'll need to teach the grade you have in mind in the state you plan to teach in.

PRE-K

It's true that math teachers are not routinely hired for work at preschools. However, if you want to work with young children and you love mathematics, there's no reason your math skills cannot be put to good use. Your degree would be in early childhood education, but you might choose to minor in or complete a concentration in mathematics. With this background, you would be in a position to instill an interest in the math around them to the youngest of learners. It might be through counting games or the comparison of one object with another. Whichever method you choose

As a math teacher, you can pass on your love of math to a new generation.

would provide your students with a strong background for future learning.

ELEMENTARY SCHOOL

Elementary schools do not always have teachers who are exclusively math teachers. Very often all of the teachers in a grade teach some level of math. If you decide to pursue a career in elementary school math, you would teach a variety of subjects. With a specialization or emphasis in math, you might be the lead teacher in math for the grade you teach.

To become a math teacher in grades K–5 (in some states it is grades K–8), you will need to earn a bachelor of arts in education (B.A.Ed.). The first two years of your degree will be spent on general classes—usually in the liberal arts. The second two years will combine classes in your area of emphasis—such as math—with student teaching opportunities, education classes, and classes on child development. For an emphasis in math, some of the classes you might take include number sense and theory, discrete mathematics, and mathematics for teachers.

NATIONAL BOARD CERTIFICATION

National board certification is the gold standard—the one that other standards are compared to—of teaching excellence. Teachers who earn national board certification in their subject area meet very difficult requirements that were set by

(continued on the next page)

(continued from the previous page)

fellow teachers. Because board certification is so respected, teachers who achieve it often receive bonuses or raises. They are also often chosen for leadership positions in their schools or school districts.

Board certification is available in twenty-five areas, for teachers of pre-K through twelfth grade. Teachers going through the certification process are able to apply what they learn in the classroom. They also have the opportunity to interact with other teaching professionals. You can see on the board certification site (http://boardcertifiedteachers.org/about-certification) that the four things required for certification are "a written assessment of content knowledge, reflection on student work samples, video and analysis of teaching practice, and documented impact and accomplishments as a teaching professional."

MIDDLE SCHOOL

Middle school teachers instruct students in grades six through eight. At some middle schools, math teachers teach only math classes. At many others, all teachers teach all subjects. Many middle schools offer classes in algebra and geometry. Your math knowledge would go a long way in making these subjects interesting and understandable to your students.

To become a middle school teacher, you will earn either a B.A.Ed. in elementary education or in secondary education, depending upon your program and the licensing requirements of your state. Once again, a portion of your coursework will be devoted to a general curriculum, a portion will be devoted to education classes, a portion will be spent student teaching, and a portion will be spent taking classes in mathematics.

HIGH SCHOOL

Those teaching grades nine through twelve will require a degree in secondary education. It will be similar to that pursued by middle school teachers who require that same degree to teach grades six through eight. Once again, coursework will include that required

Female math teachers have the opportunity to influence girls by leading academic clubs and other empowering activities.

for a general degree, along with coursework about teaching and adolescent development. Student teaching experience is also part of the curriculum leading to the degree.

THE PRESIDENTIAL AWARDS FOR EXCELLENCE IN MATHEMATICS AND SCIENCE TEACHING

The Presidential Awards for Excellence in Mathematics and Science Teaching (PAEMST) have been awarded to more than 4,300 teachers of grades K–12 math, science, and computer science since 1983. Teachers from the fifty states and four U.S. jurisdictions are eligible. To earn the award, teachers must be nominated and pass review by a selection committee at the state level and review by the National Science Foundation (NSF) before being chosen by the OSTP (Office of Science and Technology Policy). The president of the United States personally presents the awards, which include a certificate and $10,000 from the NSF.

According to the PAEMST site, award-winning teachers "develop and implement a high-quality instructional program that is informed by content and knowledge and enhances student learning." These education professionals are role models in their schools and communities who are dedicated to bringing the best practices in science and math education to future generations.

The mathematics courses you will take for a mathematics emphasis at the secondary level will include algebra, geometry, calculus, statistics, and trigonometry. It will be your task to bring these subjects to life for your future students. At the high school level, you may also have the opportunity to be a club adviser for groups that are interested in robotics, math competitions, or other related areas.

COLLEGE

Those teaching math at the college level have advanced degrees in mathematics. They have usually

Teaching math at the college level requires an advanced degree in mathematics. It's an opportunity to work with students who have a passion for math.

worked as teachers' assistants (TAs) while pursuing their own master's degree in mathematics. They are not formally trained as educators but have either majored in math as undergraduates or majored in another subject for their undergraduate degree before going on to pursue an advanced degree in mathematics.

A master's degree will be enough to earn you a position at many community colleges and colleges, but it's possible it will not be enough to earn you a position at the university you have your heart set on. For that university, you may need to have a doctorate in math. The best course of action is to learn about different mathematics departments. What do they require for entry-level positions? What is required for advancement? What will give you the most flexibility and greatest opportunities in the future?

THEORETICAL AND APPLIED MATHEMATICS: USING MATH TO IMAGINE POSSIBILITIES AND SOLVE PROBLEMS

Theoretical and applied mathematics are two fields that require graduate study. Theoretical, also known as pure, mathematicians are most likely to hold positions in university mathematics departments where a Ph.D. is a likely requirement. They explore numbers and mathematical concepts at the most esoteric level.

Applied mathematicians must also complete graduate work, but a master's degree may be sufficient. These professionals are generally employed by private business and government agencies. Applied mathematicians use their creativity and facility with numbers and mathematical concepts to solve real-world problems in a variety of fields.

Maryam Mirzakhani, pictured here with her fellow award recipients, is the first woman to be awarded the Fields Medal. It is known as "the Nobel Prize of Mathematics."

THEORETICAL MATHEMATICS

Theoretical mathematicians strive to solve math problems that have so far gone without a solution. Many theoretical mathematicians work in a university or research environment where they are actively engaged in teaching mathematics at the graduate level. They also push the boundaries of what we know about numbers and the way they work. They may even introduce a new type of math. Theoretical mathematicians are the professionals who provide the tools that are needed to solve the problems of the day.

In the mid-seventeenth century, there were many questions that could not be answered with the mathematics of the time. Sir Isaac Newton and Gottfried Leibniz, working independently, created the mathematics that is now known as infinitesimal

MARYAM MIRZAKHANI

Stanford University professor Maryam Mirzakhani is proof positive that women can excel in math. In August 2014 she became the first woman to ever receive the Fields Medal—the most prestigious honor in mathematics. Also known as the "Nobel Prize of Mathematics," it was awarded for her work on Riemann surfaces and their moduli.

In an interview for the Clay Mathematics Institute 2013 Annual Report, Mirzakhani spoke about her education and her interest in mathematics. She said, "As a kid, I dreamt of becoming a writer. My most exciting pastime was reading novels; in fact, I would read anything I could find. I never thought I would pursue mathematics before my last year in high school."

Born in Iran in 1977, Mirzakhani's first memory of mathematics was the "beautiful solution" that eighteenth-century mathematician Carl Friedrich Gauss used to solve the problem of adding numbers from 1 to 100, as shared with her by her brother.

calculus. (Newton is generally credited with being eight years ahead of Leibniz.) Today calculus is considered to be an essential mathematical discipline.

Why would it be necessary to create an entirely new type of math? According to *From Quarks to Quasars*, Newton needed a new type of math to prove the validity of his theory that the orbits of planets were ellipses because they were actually sections of cones. He also needed a form of math that would allow him to prove that the speed of an object increases every second. He understood the concepts he wanted to prove because he was a physicist. He knew his reasoning fit within the principles of physics. He created infinitesimal calculus to fit his purpose. Calculus is certainly not the last of the new disciplines that will be introduced in mathematics. In fact, there are still mathematical problems that have not been solved—even with the use of super computers. Perhaps those solutions require new disciplines of math.

To prepare for work in theoretical mathematics, you must build the best possible knowledge base by taking as many math classes as you can. You will likely require a Ph.D. Your theoretical work will expand what is known about mathematics and create tools to solve problems, many of which will be intellectual problems without a real-world application. However, as is the case with calculus, the math you create for one purpose may ultimately be used to solve pressing problems in the future.

APPLIED MATHEMATICS

Applied mathematicians use existing mathematics to solve problems in other fields. They work with professionals in engineering and physics, epidemiology and finance, to name a few. The problems they solve have real-world applications. Suppose an engineer wanted to build a prosthetic limb specifically for the purpose of running. With applied mathematics, existing fields of math could be used to create preliminary specifications for the prototype. At each milestone in the project, the mathematics could be refined. By the end of the

Studying stock performance information is one example of a career in applied mathematics.

process, not only would there be a new type of prosthetic but a new use for math as well.

A career in applied mathematics might be just right for you if you enjoy problem solving and working with others to bring mathematical concepts to real-world situations. It's one thing to know the formula for acceleration and another to hear about an engineering problem and recognize that the necessary approach to a solution might come from this simple formula. In the same way, it's one thing to know that the flu spreads through contact with droplets—think coughing and sneezing—but another to be able to create a formula or model that will accurately predict the spread of the flu so that public health officials can prepare to meet the needs of those who will require treatment.

Your first step is to take as many high school math classes as you can. In college, earn a B.S. degree in applied mathematics. With your B.S., you can work in the private or public sector, so be sure

NUMB3RS

When's the last time you saw a woman mathematician as a main character? For that matter, when was the last time you saw a male mathematician as a main character? It's safe to say that women in mathematics are not often portrayed favorably in the media.

From 2005 to 2010, the television program *Numb3rs* featured mathematical prodigy Charlie Eppes as he used applied mathematics to help his FBI agent brother solve real-world crimes. Charlie often sought input from female graduate student Amita Ramanujan and his mentor, Professor Larry Fleinhardt.

Numb3rs is significant because Ramanujan is shown to be a highly capable mathematician. She advances from completing her degree in computer science and writing her thesis on combinatorics to gaining a professorship and deciding to pursue a second Ph.D.—this one in astrophysics. She also receives a prestigious prize for her dissertation and is chosen by Fleinhardt to assist him with his work on the Higgs boson.

to find opportunities to learn about the fields that you'd like to work with—fields like engineering and finance, for instance. You might find a job on Wall Street, modeling the behavior of a particular stock

These scientists will use their math skills to collect and analyze data about air quality in Colorado.

or sector of the market. You might also find a job for a government agency that is tasked with predicting long-term weather trends or demographic changes. The main thing is that your work will combine your love of math with the opportunity to solve problems.

OPERATIONS RESEARCH AND OPTIMIZATION ENGINEERING: MATH TO THE RESCUE

Operations research and optimization engineering are two career fields that require a strong foundation in mathematics. In each of these fields, that math is put to use in solving problems about the best use of limited resources. In operations research, the decisions are often made at the management level and concern the allocation of resources. Optimization engineering looks at the engineering process to determine where the greatest efficiencies can be gained.

OPERATIONS RESEARCH

Those who work in the field of operations research use their mathematical backgrounds to create theories and models that will result in the greatest output for the least input. Also known as business analytics, the field is defined by the NYU Stern website as "the study of data through statistical and operations analysis, the formation of predictive models, application of optimization techniques . . ." The end result is a decision-making process that is based upon a deep understanding of the results of prior decisions.

A business analyst presents her findings to the management team. She has used statistical analysis to reach her conclusions.

The particular decision under discussion will determine the exact statistics and data that will be used in the model. The model will allow for different assumptions to be "tried on" by varying the inputs. It is up to the business analyst to interpret the output from the model and to present her findings to the management team.

In addition to a strong background in mathematics and business, a business analyst will need an MBA. This degree, the master in business administration, focuses on accounting, finance, marketing, and business strategy. The MBA in business analytics includes coursework on modeling and interpretation of statistics, including data-driven decision making.

It's important to be a good interviewer and have good people skills when you are working on a business analysis project.

Business analysts do not necessarily have a great deal of management experience. Their value lies in their ability to understand business operations by "reading" the numbers. Internships in a variety of businesses would be ideal for someone pursuing a career in this field, in order to have a deep sense of the underlying interrelationships of different parts of the business. If this is not possible, thorough interviews with seasoned managers or the individuals within the various parts of the company will help to gain the necessary foundation for the interpretation of the data.

Another way to gain the necessary understanding is to look through prior years' results to gain an appreciation for any cycles in the business, as well as the ways in which the different departments or divisions perform individually and as a whole. The numbers will tell you a story, but the business analyst will need a solid background in the business and industry to go along with her skill with numbers. Another way to gain this background is to join an association representing the industry of the company, read trade journals, and attend conferences.

THE INSTITUTE FOR OPERATIONS RESEARCH AND MANAGEMENT SCIENCES

The Institute for Operations Research and Management Sciences (INFORMS) is the largest society in the world for professionals in operations research (O.R.), management science, and analytics. Its goal is to support the learning needs of its members over the course of their careers.

INFORMS publishes a number of peer-reviewed journals that include case studies and describe the latest in O.R. practice, holds national and international conferences, and provides certification and continuing education opportunities, as well as podcasts on topics of interest to members.

Since its founding in 1952, INFORMS has grown to be an important organization in the field of analytics. Its membership includes Nobel laureates and Ph.D.s from respected organizations. This organization has student chapters, a magazine for students, and a student information center that includes information about internships and financial aid for graduate programs and research. There is also important information for those interested in a career in analytics/operations research.

OPTIMIZATION ENGINEERING

Those pursuing careers in optimization engineering must have strong analytical skills. They will use these skills when considering the best design for a product or the best manufacturing process to be used in creating the product. There are many ways a product can be produced, but not all ways are equally efficient. Some are more labor intensive than others. Some leave behind more waste, and since not all waste represents the same amount of money wasted, not all waste is created equal.

To optimize a process, all of the inputs must be quantified and considered. Then the costs of those inputs must be compared. It's not a straightforward process. It's possible that a plant in one part of the country might find more workers available than a plant located in another part of the country. If more labor is available, maybe the labor costs will be less. Then again, maybe a highly skilled labor pool is required. If that labor can be found more readily in one area than another, it might make sense to locate a plant in that location. It might also make the most sense to partner with local education providers to offer the types of training the manufacturer requires.

Materials are another consideration. For every unit produced, there will be some waste. What is the most efficient way to produce that product? The answer will include labor, energy costs, material costs, the cost of running the equipment—it's a lot to consider, and the role of those optimizing the engineering process is to look at each and every aspect. If labor is cheap enough, it's possible that some tasks that would be performed by a machine will be performed by a person. If the labor costs

OPTIMIZATION

Optimization is the process by which the greatest efficiency is attained from a system. For car rental companies it means having as many cars as needed on hand without having more, or fewer, cars than are needed at crunch times. For restaurants it means ordering the right amount of ingredients so that you

(continued on the next page)

For prime optimization, restaurants must make sure they order enough, but not too much, of the ingredients needed for meal service.

(continued from the previous page)

don't run out but you don't have so much left over that any will go to waste. For educational institutions it means having enough space so that all classes can meet without having empty class-rooms that require heating or overfilled classrooms that make it difficult for students to engage with the instructor. In years past, optimization problems were solved with pencil, paper, and slide rule. Today computer models are used, but to create an effective model it's still necessary to have a deep understanding of the process, as well as the different subprocesses and factors that are in play.

are prohibitive, the optimal solution may call for robotics.

A master's degree will be required for this career. It might be a master's in computation for design or in stochastic systems, to name a few possibilities. Whichever you decide upon, it will require strong analytical and reasoning skills. Coursework will include computer programming and modeling. A deep understanding of the process being designed is essential to the optimization engineer. To gain this understanding it is necessary to speak with those who have more experience in the process and to test your understanding and assumptions as you proceed.

Chapter seven

GETTING YOUR FIRST JOB

Y ou'll often hear those looking for their first job say their job search isn't going well because they can't get a job without experience, but they won't have experience until they have a job. That's true to a limited extent, but it's more important for you to recognize that good interview skills and advanced planning are things you control. The trick is for you to use this knowledge to your advantage while identifying opportunities and turning those opportunities into offers.

JOB SEARCH

A job search is comprised of all the steps you take to land a job. The more thought you give to your search at the start, the more likely you are to have a good outcome in a reasonable amount of time. For instance, there's no sense in pursuing jobs in a geographical area or work sector that you have no intention of taking. There are far more productive ways to hone your interviewing skills.

Job fairs are a great way to learn a bit about a lot of companies. As you near graduation, you may be able to interview for a job at one of these fairs.

One way to identify opportunities is to attend job fairs or recruiting visits while still in college. You might want to attend from early on so that you develop an idea of employers you admire and the type of work that interests you. Definitely participate as you near graduation. Very often interview opportunities or job offers are made to those nearing graduation.

WHAT DO ASSOCIATIONS DO?

Associations are groups that are formed to promote the interests of a particular profession or group within a profession. The AMS, MAA, and AWM are important associations for those pursuing careers in mathematics.

The American Mathematical Society (AMS) was founded in 1888 to promote mathematical research and scholarship. It supports math education and provides information for interested parties ranging from authors to researchers to students. AMS holds meetings at the regional, national, and international levels. It also provides data and information for those interested in mathematics as a profession. Membership is open to both men and women at any stage in their careers.

The Mathematical Association of America (MAA) was founded in 1915 for the purpose of promoting mathematics to those in college. It offers programs, meetings, and publications focused on supporting those who are interested in careers in mathematics. It also has materials for the professional development of teachers, along with teaching and learning resources.

The Association for Women in Mathematics (AWM) was established in 1971. Its purpose is to encourage women and girls to pursue their interest in mathematics. It holds programs, workshop, meetings, and lectures. It has student chapters, and membership is open to women and men.

RÉSUMÉ AND PORTFOLIO

A strong résumé and portfolio are vital. They're a picture of your accomplishments on paper. It's up to you to make sure you have things to include on your résumé that represent you well. That means including not only degrees and awards but also the clubs you've joined, the interests you've pursued, and the internships or volunteer work you've completed. Your goal with your résumé is for someone looking at it to know enough about you to want to meet you in person.

Not all future employers will be interested in your portfolio, but it doesn't hurt to have it with you. Your portfolio might include copies of your published articles and guidelines for projects you've given your students. The main thing is that the items in your portfolio complement what is on your résumé.

INTERVIEWING SKILLS

An interview is your chance to present yourself to the people who are in a position to hire you. The more positive an impression you make, the more likely you are to be offered a job. With that in mind, think about the things that favorably impress you when you meet someone. Someone who mumbles, looks at the ground rather than at you, is dressed for an entirely different occasion, and is generally so uncomfortable in the situation that he or she makes you uncomfortable is not someone you want to spend time with. The same is true while interviewing.The most important things to remember are:

- **Dress appropriately.** If you're not sure what to wear on an interview, speak with a career counselor or professor.
- **Be confident.** Prepare for the interview by thinking about what questions might be asked and thinking of answers that are to the point.
- **Speak up.** Don't mumble. Make eye contact. Shake hands firmly. This is your chance to show that you will be a good representative for this company.
- **Reframe negative questions.** If you're asked about the thing you regret most, answer honestly but be sure to include a sentence or two about what you learned from the experience and how you would improve upon it.

Take each interview seriously. Present yourself as a person that would represent the company in a positive way.

- **Keep it simple.** Carry a sleek tote with your résumé and portfolio. Make sure these materials are easy to pull out if you need them. You might also consider posting these things online.
- **Ask for the job.** If you want the job, ask for it at the end of the interview by telling the interviewer that what you've learned makes you confident this will be a good position for you and you'd like to have it.

AFTER THE INTERVIEW

Take the time to follow up with a thank-you note to the person who interviewed you. If you're unsure of the person's name or contact information, ask the person running the job fair or call the company where the interview took place for that information. In your thank-you, begin by thanking the person for the time spent with you, include something that you appreciated about the interview, and end by mentioning that you look forward to hearing from the interviewer soon.

NETWORKING/VOLUNTEERING/ INTERNSHIPS

Making the time to network, volunteer, or work as an intern pays off in many ways. You not only learn about the profession, industry, or company, you also make contacts along the way. These opportunities are also your very first steps to gaining the real-world experience you'll need when applying for your first job. For these reasons, it's very important that you treat each "gig" as a potential interview. You do this by acting appropriately and treating meetings you attend and work you do as seriously as you would treat an actual job. Some of the contacts you make may offer to serve as a reference for you. Others may not offer but will readily agree when asked. Be sure to keep a list of the people you work with as you volunteer or work as an intern, along with contact information for those people in case you are asked to list people you have worked for when you apply for a job.

Volunteer. Join organizations affiliated with your future profession. The more you know about the industry, the better able you'll be to bring value to your company.

BECOMING A VALUED EMPLOYEE

Be professional from the start. Be on time. Be conscientious. Do your best work. Ask questions if you're not sure what is expected. The more you prove yourself to be a reliable and proficient employee, the more valuable you will be.

Show that you are a team player by doing your part to make any group you work with a successful group.

Show that you are a leader by assuming a leadership role when it is appropriate for you. How will you know? You will have the skills that are needed to see the bigger picture and articulate that to the team while keeping the team on task.

Continue your education by reading journals and attending lectures. As you become familiar with the latest news in your profession, you bring that knowledge back to your company.

The most important part of being a valued employee is doing your job thoroughly and with a good attitude. Be the employee you would like to have.

Chapter eight

LIFELONG LEARNING: ADVANCING UP THE LADDER

L ifelong learners are people with active and curious minds. They understand that new developments are happening in their field and they want to know about it. They may pursue certification, take an active role in their professional association, or serve as mentor to those just starting out. They may stay informed by attending conferences, reading journals, or a combination of both. Whichever they choose, their goal is to stay informed and current in their field.

Upon earning your undergraduate or graduate degree, in some fields you will be required to complete a specified number of continuing education units (CEU) each year. This is especially likely if your profession requires a license of any kind. CEUs are offered by associations and schools that have programs in your area of study. The coursework for CEUs is designed to keep you informed of new findings or to provide you with the opportunity for additional training in your field.

PROFESSIONAL CERTIFICATIONS

Professional certification can be earned in nearly every field. Certification is earned as a result of additional study in your area of expertise. In finance alone, the CMA, CFP, and CFA are just three possibilities. The certified management accountant (CMA) certification indicates that you have a thorough knowledge of the use of accounting and financial management skills. The certified financial planner (CFP) designation is earned for your work in financial planning. The chartered financial analyst (CFA) certification will prepare you for a career in investment analysis and institutional money management.

You can learn about the certifications that will make a difference in your career by consulting the website of the professional association for your field or speaking with a professional in your career. You can also learn about these certifications as a student member of the professional association related to your career field.

CONTINUING EDUCATION/ PROFESSIONAL DEVELOPMENT

Many licensing organizations require continuing education units (CEUs) to be earned each year. These CEUs indicate that you have taken the required coursework to remain current in your field. The number of CEUs varies by the type of license you hold. If a class you intend to take will count toward your CEUs, it should state it in the course description. If you're uncertain, check with the agency that requires the CEUs before you take the course.

Conferences often offer workshops on topics of interest to attendees. Check the agenda for conferences near you and find the ones that have programs that interest you.

Professional development includes courses you take to improve your skillset, whether or not the course counts toward a certification or your required CEUs. You might decide that some knowledge of computer programming would help you in your career. Taking a programming course would be an example of professional development. Public speaking classes and presentation software classes are two other examples. You may find that your company will reimburse you for the cost of these classes.

WHY GO TO CONFERENCES?

Conferences are educational and networking opportunities geared around a specific topic or field. They are often sponsored by associations, although they can also be sponsored by universities, nonprofits, or corporations.

Conferences are likely to offer workshops on topics of interest to the attendees. These workshops may offer continuing education credit. The material covered may be part of a certification process or simply a way to learn about the latest research.

Some professionals attend conferences for the many opportunities to network, or meet others who share similar interests. Sometimes these meetings lead to opportunities for positions that are open. At the very least, they provide an opportunity to speak about the conference theme or related topics with people who are knowledgeable about and engaged in those topics.

Students also attend conferences as a way to learn more about their field of interest. There they may meet students from other universities. They may also learn about hiring trends, internships, or other educational opportunities.

All in all, a conference that is about a topic of interest to you can be a terrific way to get the latest information and speak with people at various stages of their careers about the work they do.

PROFESSIONAL ASSOCIATIONS

Professional associations provide many opportunities to further your learning. There are workshops, conferences, seminars, and classes. You can attend any or all of these,

There are many opportunities to volunteer at conferences. One way is to make a presentation or teach a class. You might also be on a panel with others in your field.

as well as volunteer to present at these events. You can also join one of the many committees working to prepare educational materials or the events themselves. By taking an active role, you will be working with others in your field of interest. This will give you a chance to speak with them about their work and interests, as well as to speak about your interests and work.

Professional associations usually have branches at colleges. These branches require support and resources from the association. By acting as a liaison, you will be aware of the latest research and findings.

Professional associations also often have active chat boards where their members discuss their work. Any of these opportunities will add to your knowledge while keeping you current in your field.

MENTORING

Mentoring requires you to take an active interest in the career of someone who is junior to you. As a mentor, you meet with the person, listen to what she is working on, and give appropriate comments and suggestions. You might help your mentee to get an internship or first job. You might offer advice on how to better advocate

Mentoring is a way for you to share what you know with someone who is just starting out.

for herself. You might offer suggestions for courses to take, professional organizations to join, or journals that are worth the time to read.

As a mentor, you will need to keep abreast of changes in your field. Part of this may be through classes and reading you do on your own. Part of it may be in the form of information you learn from the person you are mentoring and others who are just starting out. Much of it will be the result of the interactions you have with the people you consult in your role as mentor.

JOURNALS

Journals are magazines with a purpose. Some are very technical in nature. All are focused on a central theme. One journal might be about investment analysis. Another might be about operations research. Whichever it is, a reader can expect articles on topics related to this subject matter and geared toward a professional audience. By reading professional journals in your field, you will learn about the issues being discussed, the major players in the field, and the types of research being done to address concerns.

It's a good idea to begin reading journals while you are in college or even in high school. (Very often you can join a professional association as a student and subscribe at a reduced rate.) The more issues you read, the more familiar you will become with the vocabulary of your new field and the type of work that is being done.

Glossary

ACCESSIBLE Describes an idea or place that is easy to understand or reach.

ALGORITHM A set of step-by-step instructions.

ALLOCATION The way a whole is distributed in portions.

BACHELOR'S DEGREE A degree that is earned from a four-year college.

CIPHER A way of writing a secret message.

CRYPTOGRAM A message that is written in code.

ENCRYPT To put information into a cipher or code so that it cannot be easily read.

ENTITY Something that exists independently, such as a business or person.

ESOTERIC Specialized and understood by a small number of people.

GRADUATE LEVEL Describes coursework that is done after a college degree is earned.

INTERNSHIP An opportunity to work, often without pay, for the purpose of gaining experience.

MASTER'S DEGREE A degree that is earned after a bachelor's degree.

PH.D. A degree that is earned after a master's degree.

PREJUDICE Beliefs or opinions about a subject or person without regard for the facts.

PROWESS Skill or expertise in a subject or field.

REAL-WORLD Describes a question or solution that is related to a day-to-day problem.

RIGOROUS Physically or intellectually challenging or demanding.

STEM Acronym for the fields of science, technology, engineering, and mathematics.

STEREOTYPE A perception or belief about a type of person that is shared by many but not necessarily accurate.

THEOREM A mathematical statement that is proven based on established statements.

For More Information

Advantage Testing Foundation
210 East 86th Street, Suite 601
New York, NY 20028
Attn: Math Prize for Girls
(212) 744-8800
Website: http://mathprize.atfoundation.org
The Advantage Testing Foundation sponsors the Math
    Prize for Girls each year as a way to inspire young
    women in high school to become the mathematical
    leaders of tomorrow. The competition awards the
    largest monetary math prize for girls in the world.
    This site has info, a blog, and a PBS documentary
    on the 2010 Math Prize.

American Association of University Women
1111 Sixteenth Street NW
Washington, DC 20036
(202) 785-7700
Website: http://www.aauw.org
The American Association of University Women
    (AAUW) has a list of STEM programs for girls
    listed under the "What We Do" tab.

American Mathematical Society
201 Charles Street
Providence, RI 02904-2294
(401) 455-4000
Website: http://www.ams.org
The American Mathematical Society (AMS) serves
    the national and international mathematical com-
    munity through its publications, meetings, advo-
    cacy, and other programs.

Association for Women in Mathematics
11240 Waples Mill Road, Suite 200
Fairfax, VA 22030
(703) 934-0163
Website: https://sites.google.com/site/awmmath/
    home
The Association for Women in Mathematics (AWM)
    was founded in 1971. Its mission is to encour-
    age women and girls to study mathematics and
    to have active careers in mathematics. This site
    has a Girls in Math and Science page with lots of
    resources and info.

Canadian Mathematical Society
209 – 1725 St. Laurent Boulevard
Ottawa, ON K1G 3V4
Canada
(613) 733-2662
Website: http://cms.math.ca
The Canadian Mathematical Society is dedicated to
    the promotion of advancement in mathematics
    in Canada. It also sponsors events such as
    Connecting Women in Mathematics Across
    Canada and summer math camps. Find the
    details on this site. Info about Math Team
    Canada is also at this site.

Engineers Canada
180 Elgin Street, Suite 1100
Ottawa, ON K2P 2K3
Canada
(613) 232-2474

Website: http://www.engineerscanada.ca
Engineers Canada regulates the practice of
    engineering in Canada. It is the licensing
    organization for engineers in Canada.
    Information about careers and educational
    opportunities as well as events of interest to
    those interested in engineering are on this site.

IEEE Women in Engineering
3 Park Avenue, 17th Floor
New York, NY 10016
(212) 419-7900
Website: http://www.ieee.org/membership_
    services/membership/women/
IEEE Women in Engineering (WIE) is the largest
    international professional organization
    dedicated to promoting women engineers and
    scientists. It is also dedicated to inspiring
    girls around the world to follow their interests
    in engineering. This site has information about
    careers and educational opportunities.

Mathematical Association of America
1529 18th Street NW
Washington, DC 20036
(800) 741-9415
Website: http://www.maa.org
The Mathematical Association of America (MAA) has a
    range of programs. It also sponsors the American
    Mathematics Competitions (AMC). You can find
    info about that and other competitions on the site.

Sally Ride Science
9171 Towne Centre Drive, Suite 350
San Diego, CA 92122
(800) 561-5161
Website: https://sallyridescience.com
Sally Ride Science was founded by Dr. Sally Ride,
    America's first woman astronaut in space. Its
    mission is to inspire girls to pursue careers in
    STEM fields such as math. This site has links to
    books and programs that will be of interest to
    girls. It also has info on how to start a Sally Ride
    Science Festival.

Society for Industrial and Applied Mathematics
3600 Market Street, 6th Floor
Philadelphia, PA 19104-2688
(215) 382-9800
Website: http://siam.org
The mission of the Society for Industrial and Ap-
    plied Mathematics (SIAM) is to build cooperation
    between the STEM fields through their publica-
    tions, research, and community.

Society of Women Engineers
203 N. LaSalle Street, Suite 1675
Chicago, IL 60601
(877) 793-4636
Website: http://societyofwomenengineers.swe.org
The Society of Women Engineers (SWE) is the first
    society dedicated to the advancement of women
    in engineering.

WEBSITES

Because of the changing nature of Internet links, Rosen Publishing has developed an online list of websites related to the subject of this book. This site is updated regularly. Please use this link to access this list:

http://www.rosenlinks.com/TECH/Math

For Further Reading

Adler, Charles L. *Wizards, Aliens, and Starships: Physics and Math in Fantasy and Science Fiction*. Princeton, NJ: Princeton University Press, 2014.

Barnes-Svarney, Patricia L., and Thomas E. Svarney. *The Handy Math Answer Book*. Canton, MI: Visible Ink Press, 2012.

Cantú, Norma Elia. *Paths to Discovery: Autobiographies from Chicanas with Careers in Science, Mathematics, and Engineering*. Los Angeles, CA: UCLA Chicano Studies Research Center Press, 2008.

Farr, J. Michael. *Top 100 Computer and Technical Careers: Your Complete Guidebook to Major Jobs in Many Fields at All Training Levels*. Indianapolis, IN: JIST Pub., 2009.

Frize, Monique, Peter R. D. Frize, and Nadine Faulkner. *The Bold and the Brave: A History of Women in Science and Engineering*. Ottawa, ON: University of Ottawa Press, 2009.

Gibilisco, Stan. *Everyday Math Demystified*. New York, NY: McGraw-Hill, 2013.

Institute for Career Research. *Engineering and Technical Careers in Green Energy*. Chicago, IL: Institute for Career Research, 2011.

JIST Works, Inc. *Stem Careers: Guide to Occupations in Science, Technology, Engineering, and Mathematics*. Indianapolis, IN: JIST Works, 2011.

Layne, Margaret. *Women in Engineering* (Pioneers and Trailblazers). Reston, VA: ASCE Press, 2009.

Layne, Margaret E. *Women in Engineering: Professional Life*. Reston, VA: ASCE Press, 2009.

Mahaney, Ian F. *The Math of Baseball*. New York, NY: Powerkids Press, 2012.

McKellar, Danica. *Girls Get Curves: Geometry Takes Shape*. New York, NY: Hudson Street Press, 2012.

McKellar, Danica. *Hot X: Algebra Exposed*. New York, NY: Hudson Street Press, 2010.

McKellar, Danica. *Kiss My Math: Showing Pre-Algebra Who's Boss*. New York, NY: Hudson Street Press, 2008.

McKellar, Danica. *Math Doesn't Suck: How to Survive Year 6 Through Year 9 Math Without Losing Your Mind or Breaking a Nail*. London, England: Penguin, 2010.

Parkinson, Claire L., Pamela S. Millar, and Michelle Thaller. *Women of Goddard: Careers in Science, Technology, Engineering & Mathematics*. Greenbelt, MD: NASA Goddard Space Flight Center, 2011.

Polster, Burkard, and Marty Ross. *Math Goes to the Movies*. Baltimore, MD: Johns Hopkins University Press, 2012.

Potter, Lawrence. *Mathematics Minus Fear: How to Make Math Fun and Beneficial to Your Everyday Life*. New York, NY: Pegasus Books, 2012.

Rosser, Sue Vilhauer. *Breaking into the Lab: Engineering Progress for Women in Science*. New York, NY: New York University Press, 2012.

Shapiro, Lauren J. *Easy Math: Poems*. Louisville, KY: Sarabande Books, 2013.

American Statistical Association. "How Do I Become a Statistician." January 1, 2014. Retrieved October 20, 2014 (http://www.amstat. org/careers/howdoibecomeastatistician.cfm).

American Statistical Association. "What Do Statisticians Do?" January 1, 2014. Retrieved October 20, 2014 (http://www.amstat.org/ careers/whatdostatisticiansdo.cfm).

American Statistical Association. "What Is Statistics?" January 1, 2014. Retrieved October 20, 2014 (http://www.amstat.org/careers/ whatisstatistics.cfm).

American Statistical Association. "Which Industries Employ Statisticians?" January 1, 2014. Retrieved October 20, 2014 (http://www.amstat.org/careers/ whichindustriesemploystatisticians.cfm).

Axelrod, Jim. "Dance Program Shows Girls and Math Can Add Up." *CBS Evening News*, May 27, 2014. Retrieved July 25, 2014 (http://www.cbsnews. com/news/dance-program-shows-girls-and-math-can-add-up).

Boscia, Ted. "Program Teaches Girls Engineering via Apparel Design." *Cornell Chronicle*, August 6, 2013. Retrieved July 25, 2014 (http://www.news. cornell.edu/stories/2013/08/program-teaches-girls-engineering-apparel-design).

Corporate Planning and Policy Directorate Natural Sciences and Engineering Research Council of Canada. "Women in Science and Engineering." 2010. Retrieved July 25, 2014 (http://www

.nserc-crsng.gc.ca/_doc/Reports-Rapports/ Women_Science_Engineering_e.pdf).

Engineers Without Borders, "Our History - Engineers Without Borders." 2013. Retrieved July 25, 2014 (http://www.ewb-usa.org/our-story/our-history).

Investopedia. "The Alphabet Soup of Financial Certifications." January 1, 2014. Retrieved September 15, 2014 (http://www.investopedia .com/articles/01/101001.asp).

Park, Alice. "Girls Beat Boys in Every Subject, and They Have for a Century." *Time*, April 29, 2014. Retrieved July 25, 2014 (http://time.com/81355/ girls-beat-boys-in-every-subject-and-they-have -for-a-century).

University of Maryland University College. "Major in Finance." January 1, 2014. Retrieved October 19, 2014 (http://www.umuc.edu/academic-programs/ bachelors-degrees/finance-major.cfm).

University of Nebraska. "All Girls/All Math." 2014. Retrieved July 25, 2014 (http://www.math.unl .edu/programs/agam).

Index

ABOUT THE AUTHOR

Gina Hagler is a published author and writer. She blogs about science and technology at http://www.ginahagler.com. Her books for Springer Verlag are about engineering-related topics. She has taught and led training workshops in the STEM fields and developed curriculum for a variety of STEM courses. She is a member of the National Association of Science Writers (NASW), as well as the American Society of Journalists and Authors (ASJA) and the Society of Environmental Journalists (SEJ).

PHOTO CREDITS

Cover © iStockphoto.com/SimmiSimons; cover and interior pages background image © iStockphoto.com/HandmadePictures; cover and interior pages text banners © iStockphoto.com/slav; p. 5 Imeh Akpanudosen/Getty Images; p. 8 GraphicaArtis/Hulton Archive/Getty Images; pp. 10, 64 racorn/Shutterstock.com; p. 12 Andres Rodriguez/Hemera/Thinkstock; p. 15 bikeriderlondon/ Shutterstock.com; p. 17 Wellcome Library, London/CC BY 4.0; p. 19 © iStockphoto.com/Christopher Futcher; p. 23 Blend Images/SuperStock; p. 26 U.S. Navy photo by MC3 Christopher K. Hwang; p. 27 Bletchley Park Trust/SSPL/Getty Images; p. 30 Creatas/Thinkstock; p. 33 © iStockphoto.com/Lokibaho; p. 35 © iStockphoto.com/andresrimaging; p. 38 Sipa/AP Images; p. 41 © David Young-Wolff/Photo Edit; p. 43 RJ Sangosti/The Denver Post/Getty Images; p. 45 Klaus Tiedge/Blend Images/ Thinkstock; p. 46 Andreas Rodriguez/iStock/Thinkstock; p. 49 wavebreakmedia/Shutterstock.com; p. 52 Robert Nickelsberg/ Getty Images; p. 55 Stephen Coburn/Shutterstock.com; p. 57 © iStockphoto.com/MachineHeadz; p. 61 © Dennis MacDonald/ PhotoEdit; p. 63 lightpoet/Shutterstock.com.

Designer: Nicole Russo; Editor: Christine Poolos